香港國際詩歌之夜 2013
INTERNATIONAL POETRY NIGHTS IN HONG KONG

編輯 Editors

北島 Bei Dao

陳嘉恩 Shelby K. Y. Chan

方梓勳 Gilbert C. F. Fong

柯夏智 Lucas Klein

馬德松 Christopher Mattison

藍藍
Lan Lan

目錄 Contents

1 短句 6
Short Lines

2 真實 8
Vérité

3 永遠裏有…… 10
Inside Eternity …

4 詩人無用 12
Poets Are Useless

5 震驚 16
Shock

6 火車，火車 18
Train, Train

7 一切的理由 22
Reason for Everything

8 你是 24
You Are

9 一般定律 26
Standard Law

10 歇晌 28
Siesta

11 風 30
Wind

12 野葵花 32
Wild Sunflower

13 談論人生 34
Discussing Life

14 驚 36
Startle

15 釘子 38
Nails

16 山楂樹 48
Hawthorn Tree

17 玫瑰 50
Rose

18 在大師的客廳裏 52
In Maestro's Living Room

19 影子 54
Shadow

20 詩人的工作 56
A Poet's Work

1 短句

已經晚了。在我
迷路之前。

我喜歡這個——
瘋狂。這最安靜的。

可以拖著你所經歷的來愛我但恐懼於
　　用它認識我。

我將是你獲得世界的一種方式：
每樣事物都不同因而是
　　同一種。

Short Lines

Already late. Before I
get lost.

I like this—
madness. The stillest.

You drag in experience to love me, yet fear
  using it to know me.

I'll be a way you reach for the world:
everything is different, so it's
  the same.

(Translated by Fiona Sze-Lorrain)

2 真實

死人知道我們的謊言。在清晨
林間的鳥知道風。

果實知道大地之血的灌溉
哭聲知道高腳杯的體面。

喉嚨間的石頭意味著亡靈在場
喝下它！猛獸的車輪需要它的潤滑——

碾碎人，以及牙齒企圖說出的真實。
世界在盲人腦袋的裂口裏扭動

……黑暗從那裏來

Vérité

The dead know our lies. At dawn
forest birds know the wind.

Fruits know irrigation by the land's blood
Cries know the dignity of a wine glass.

Stones in my throat evoke dead souls
Drink it! Wheels of beasts' carts need the grease—

crushing man, and the truth that teeth try to speak.
The world twists in the cracks of a blind skull

… where the dark arrives

(Translated by Fiona Sze-Lorrain)

3 永遠裏有……

永遠裏有幾場雨。一陣陣微風；
永遠裏有無助的悲苦，黃昏落日時
　　茫然的愣神；

有蘋果花在死者的墓地紛紛飄落；
有歌聲，有萬家燈火的淒涼；

有兩株麥穗，一朵雲

將它們放進你的蔚藍。

Inside Eternity …

A few bands of rain inside eternity. Breezes;
forlorn inside eternity, at dusk the sunset
　　　　a blank gaze;

apple blossoms fall in a graveyard;
singing, desolate myriad city lights;

two ears of wheat, a cloud

put them into your sky blue.

(Translated by Fiona Sze-Lorrain)

4 詩人無用

無用的字，無用的眼淚
無用的瘟疫在壯大它的無用
無用淩辱被它毀掉的
　　單數的人

水是淚滴，米飯是沙粒
饅頭是堅硬的石塊
臥室是深淵，廚房是黑暗
每一次呼吸都是被死亡追趕的哀號

無用於最漂亮的面具
無用於一張被劣質水泥板砸碎的
女人的臉，雨水中白皙大腿的腐爛

一場地震加深了地獄的血盆大口
無用的痛哭沖刷迷惘的眼
誰能看見活著的可恥習慣？

沒救的人，依然在喝死人的血
猶如這幾行文字
在加深我的恥辱、窒息——

寫下它：

罪責仍在繼續……

Poets Are Useless

Useless words, useless tears
Useless plague expanding its uselessness
Uselessness insults each and every one
it has destroyed

Water is a teardrop, rice a grain of sand
A steamed bun is solid stone
A bedroom an abyss, a kitchen the darkness
Each breath is an anguished howl chased by death

Useless to the loveliest mask
Useless to a woman's face smashed by weak cement
slabs, a fair thigh decaying in the rain

An earthquake deepens the bloody maw of hell
Useless wails cleanse perplexed eyes
Who can see the shameful habit: an ignoble life?

Hopeless men, still drinking blood from the dead
Like these lines
deepening my disgrace, my suffocation—

write it down:
Guilt still goes on …

(Translated by Fiona Sze-Lorrain)

5 震驚

仇恨是酸的，腐蝕自己的獨腿
惡是地獄，裝著惡的身軀。

眼珠在黑白中轉動
猶如人在善惡裏運行：

——我用它看見枝頭的白霜
美在低處慢慢結冰

居然。

Shock

Hatred is sour, corroding its one leg
Evil is hell, packed with evil bodies.

The eyeball rotates in black and white
like man shifting between good and evil:

—I use this notion to see frost on branch tips
Beauty is slowly freezing beneath

Indeed.

(Translated by Fiona Sze-Lorrain)

6 火車，火車

黃昏把白晝運走。窗口從首都
搖落到華北的沉沉暮色中

……從這裏，到這裏。

道路擊穿大地的白楊林
閃電，會跟隨著雷
但我們的嘴已裝上安全的消聲器。

火車越過田野，這頁刪掉粗重腳印的紙。
我們晃動。我們也不再用言詞
幫助低頭的羊群，在磚窯的滾滾濃煙。

輪子慢慢滑進黑夜。從這裏
到這裏。頭頂不滅的星星
一直跟隨，這場墓地漫長的送行
在我們勇氣的狹窄鐵軌上延伸

火車。火車。離開報紙的新聞版
駛進鄉村木然的冷噤：

一個倒懸在夜空中
垂死之人的看。

Train, Train

Dusk carts day away. From the capital the window
swings down into the deep twilight of North China

… from here, to here.

A road pierces through the aspen forest
Lightning, then thunder
yet silencers have safely covered our mouths.

The train crosses the field, a page erasing clumsy
  footsteps.
We sway. We no longer use words
to help goats with bowed heads, smoke billowing from
  brick kilns.

Wheels slide slowly into night. From here
to here. Overhead, ardent stars
trail behind, this long farewell in a graveyard
stretches along the thin railway of our courage

Train. Train. Pulling out from a newshole in a journal

driving into the numb shivers of villages:
a look from the dying
hanging upside-down in the night sky.

(Translated by Fiona Sze-Lorrain)

7 一切的理由

我的唇最終要從人的關係那早年的
　　蜂巢深處被餵到一滴蜜。

不會是從花朵。
也不會是星空。

假如它們不像我的親人
它們也不會像我。

Reason for Everything

At last my lips are fed by a honey drop deep from a
  honeycomb
    kinship of an earlier time.

Not from flowers.
Nor the starry sky.

If they weren't like my kin
they aren't like me.

(Translated by Fiona Sze-Lorrain)

8 你是

秋天。你說。
（你是秋天？）

聽，楊樹的沙沙聲。
（你是楊樹的沙沙聲？）

坐在草地上。
（你是草地，或者草地是你？）

還有羊蹄甲花——
現在我看見你了，

和你帶來的它們
但你不是它們
它們不是你

楊樹的沙沙聲不是。
草地不是。還有
羊蹄甲花也不是。

You Are

autumn. You say.
(Are you autumn?)

Listen, the shuffling of poplars.
(Are you the shuffling of poplars?)

Sit on the grass.
(Are you grass, or is grass you?)

And bauhinias—
now I see you,

and those you bring along
but you are not them
they are not you

Not the shuffling of poplars.
Not grass. And
not bauhinias.

(Translated by Fiona Sze-Lorrain)

9 一般定律

緊張在清晨的一個懶腰中。
在拖鞋、吃飯和聊天的
粉紅戰壕裏。

其餘的是瘋狂。

你所知道最緊張的
已經鬆弛了。

Standard Law

Tension in a morning stretch.
In pink trenches
of slippers, eating and chatting.

The rest is madness.

The greatest stress you know
has loosened.

(Translated by Fiona Sze-Lorrain)

10 歇晌

午間。村莊慢慢沉入
　　明亮的深夜。

穿堂風掠過歇晌漢子的脊梁
躺在炕席上的母親奶著孩子
芬芳的身體與大地平行。

知了叫著。驢子在槽頭
甩動尾巴驅趕蚊蠅。

絲瓜架下，一群雛雞臥在陰影裏
間或骨碌著金色的眼珠。

這一切細小的響動——
——世界深沉的寂靜。

Siesta

Noon. The village slumps into
    a bright late night.

A draft brushes the spine of a napping man
a mother lies on a *kang* mat nursing her child
her fragrant body aligning with the earth.

Cicadas drone. At the trough a donkey
flicks its tail at mosquitoes.

Under a gourd trellis, a brood of chicks idle in the
  shade
golden eyes rolling every now and then.

These delicate sounds of movement—
—profound silence in the world.

(Translated by Fiona Sze-Lorrain)

11 風

風從他身體裏吹走一些東西。

木橋。雀舌草葉上露珠礦燈的夜晚
一隻手臂　臉　以及眼眶中
蒲公英花蕊的森林。
吹走他身體裏的峽谷。
一座空房子。和多年留在
牆壁上沉默的聲音。

風吹走他的內臟　親人的地平線。
風把他一點點掏空。
他變成沙粒　一堆粉末
　　風使他永遠活下去——

Wind

Wind blows away things from his body.

Wooden bridge. Night of miners' lamps, dewdrops on
leaves like sparrow tongues
an arm   a face   a forest
of dandelion pistils in the eyes.
Blows away the canyon in his body.
An empty house. Silent voices
left on the wall for years.

Wind blows away his organs   the horizon of
kinship.
Wind empties him little by little.
He becomes sand grains   powder
Wind lets him live on forever—

(Translated by Fiona Sze-Lorrain)

12 野葵花

野葵花到了秋天就要被
砍下頭顱。
打她身邊走過的人會突然
回來。天色已近黃昏，
她的臉，隨夕陽化為
金色的煙塵，
連同整個無邊無際的夏天。

穿越誰？穿越蕎麥花的天邊？
為憂傷所掩蓋的舊事，我
替誰又死了一次？

不真實的野葵花。不真實的
歌聲。
扎疼我胸膛的秋風的毒刺。

Wild Sunflower

Come autumn the wild sunflower head
will be chopped off.
Those who walk past her will suddenly
turn back. Dusk soon,
with sunset, her face transforms
into golden smoke,
along the vast summer.

Through whom? A horizon of buckwheat flowers?
Old past veiled in sorrow, for whom
have I died once more?

Untrue wild sunflower. Untrue
singing.
A lethal thorn of autumn wind pricks my chest.

(Translated by Fiona Sze-Lorrain)

13 談論人生

他好像在講一本什麼書。
他談論著一些人的命運。

我盯著他破舊的圓領衫出神。
我聽見窗外樹葉的沙沙聲。

我聽見他前年、去年的輕輕嗓音。
我看見窗外迅速變幻的天空。

不知何時辦公室裏暗下來。
他也沉默了很久很久。

四周多麼寧靜。
窗外傳來樹葉的沙沙聲。

Discussing Life

He seems to be lecturing on a book.
He is discussing some people's fates.

I stare transfixed at his shabby crew neck.
I hear the rustling of leaves outside.

I hear his soft voice from years past.
I see the sky fast mutating outside.

Not knowing when the office has turned dark.
He too falls into a long, long silence.

So quiet everywhere.
The rustling of leaves outside.

(Translated by Fiona Sze-Lorrain)

14 驚

你睡著
做夢　奔跑
星星在天空而大海在漲潮

所有的只是一件事
你做夢　奔跑
也許這是真的
我注視著你微微顫動的睫毛

你的手告訴我我正在成為的東西：
　　女人。
不是花
也不是匿名的詩篇
——這也是真的？
當你幫助一個女人分娩自己
我從前居然不知道
她從未出生
如此漫長地等待你今夜的口令——

Startle

You're asleep
dreaming   running
Stars in the sky as tides rise

All in one thing—
you're dreaming   running
Perhaps it's real
I watch your eyelashes tremble

Your hand tells me what I'm becoming:
        woman.
Neither a flower
nor an anonymous poem
—is this also real?
When you help a woman deliver herself
I've no idea
she was never born
waiting so long for your password in this night—

(Translated by Fiona Sze-Lorrain)

15 釘子

一

我願意走在你的後面，以便與你同享墓塚。
那裏的野草呼喚著四季，並從落葉上憐憫地收留
　　我。

二

如此安靜，聚集起整個天空的閃電。
靜默的瓦松知道——我的本質屋頂上的避雷針。

三

佩戴梔子花的人過去了。人消逝，梔子花一朵朵在
　　茶杯上燃燒。

四

生活，有多少次我被驅趕進一個句號！

五

一個中年莊稼漢的褲腳下升起了炊煙。
微風來了，最高的塔被吹成平地。

六

火石。這黑暗中不停冒煙的詞。

七

寒風吹著光禿禿的樹枝。
路燈把我變成幽靈。孩子的笑聲沉重地蓋住我的
　　臉。
牆角旋起紙屑。
我抓住它們，緊緊地——瘋狂可以是這樣平靜。
世界在孩子的笑聲中飄浮起來。打著旋。

八

自豪於自由的枷鎖可以如此堅定地對我的自由進行
　　囚禁。
在那廣袤原野裏放生了自由本身的無限。

九

還能走到哪裏？
我的字一步一步拖著我的床和我的碗。

十

打開這本書，它的高速公路試管裏淌出的墨漬。
挖掘機履帶的印刷體，土地在它日益擴大的嗥叫前
　　後退。

在它輝煌的筆杆下我們挖出我們的眼，鏟斷我們的
　　手
當昨天消失。

十一

卑賤者不被允許進入文字。
劊子手來了，揮舞著筆在你們的沉默前哆嗦。

噩夢跟著他。

十二

願你活著。永遠活著。

——一個人對仇敵的祝福。

十三

有時，一聲遙遠的哭泣，一個孤單離去的背影拋出
繩索
從深淵救出我。

我認出那張我曾無情擊打過的臉。

十四

深夜，一列細小的花朵窸窸窣窣在爬樹，沿著青色
的枝條——
當人們進入悲慘的夢寐。

十五

我的忠貞的根深扎在背叛你的泥土中。
多麼冷酷啊！

你知道，我愛你。

你生下我。

十六

我的毫無用處：

以它的一磚一瓦造出大海，並在它的快樂上面升起

　　我小屋的帆。

Nails

1

I'm willing to walk behind you, so that we may share a
burial mound.
Where wild grass summons four seasons, adopting me
by pity from fallen leaves.

2

So quiet, lightning assembled from the whole sky.
Silent orostachys know—the lightning rod on the
rooftop of my self.

3

Gone is the one who wore a gardenia. She disappears,
gardenias burn one by one above a teacup.

4

Life, many times have I been driven into a period!

5

Smoke rises from the bottom of a middle-aged
plowman's pants.

Here comes a breeze, the tallest pagoda is cast into flat land.

6

Flint. The word that keeps fuming in the dark.

7

A cold wind blows on bare branches.
Streetlights turn me into a ghost. Children's laughter drapes my face.
Scraps of paper whirl in a corner.
I grab them, tightly—madness can be this calm.
The world floats in the midst of children's laughter. Whirling.

8

Chains that boast of freedom can hold my freedom in such firm captivity.
Setting free the infinity of freedom in vast fields.

9

Where else can I go?
My words are hauling my bed and my bowl step by step.

10

Open this book, ink stains are dripping out of its freeway test tube.
Typeface of an excavator's tank tread, the soil recedes before its expanding growls.

Under its splendid pen we dig out our eyes, raze our hands
as yesterday disappears.

11

Scum are not allowed in words.
Here comes the executioner, brandishing his pen and trembling before your silence.

Nightmares stalk him.

12

May you live. Live forever.

—a blessing on one's foe.

13

Sometimes, a distant sob, a lonely departing silhouette
throws a rope
to rescue me from an abyss.

I recognize the face I once struck mercilessly.

14

Late night, a row of delicate flowers climb a tree,
swishing along green branches—
as people enter their tragic dreams.

15

My loyal roots are entrenched in mud that betrays you.
How ruthless!

You know, I love you.

You gave birth to me.

16

My utter uselessness:
with bricks and tiles it builds an ocean, raising the sail
of my cottage over its happiness.

(Translated by Fiona Sze-Lorrain)

16 山楂樹

最美的是花。粉紅色。
但如果沒有低垂的葉簇

它隱藏在蔭涼的影子深處
一道暮色裏的山谷；

如果沒有樹枝，淺褐的皮膚
像渴望抓緊泥土；

沒有風在它少年碧綠的衝動中
被月光的磁鐵吸引；

沒有走到樹下突然停住的人
他們燃燒在一起的嘴唇——！

Hawthorn Tree

Loveliest is the flower. Pink.
But were there no clusters of drooping leaves

hidden deep in its bosky shadow
a valley at dusk;

were there no branches, their beige skin
grabbing mud like desire;

no wind in its green impulse of youth
drawn to the magnet of moonlight;

no one walking to a halt under the tree
their lips burning together—!

(Translated by Fiona Sze-Lorrain)

17 玫瑰

她是禮服。離開植物學或
修辭學的戲台後
也是。

洗碗布旁過於潔白的封面。

即便沒有別的鮮花，她們
仍然是女王。

每一個都是。

被卑微加冕。

Rose

She is a gown. After leaving the stage
of botany or rhetoric
she still is—

An overly white front cover next to a dishrag.

Even if there are no other flowers, they
are still empresses.

Each of them.

Crowned by humility.

(Translated by Fiona Sze-Lorrain)

18 在大師的客廳裏

學術裏沒有血漬。平靜裏
也沒有。

深秋的菊花光著身子
在寒風裏瑟瑟發抖。

從什麼時候起，你不再
熱愛那些聰明的著述，字典裏的
偉大智慧？

你的頭髮越來越像枯萎的花瓣
在寒風中瑟瑟發抖！

In Maestro's Living Room

No bloodstains in academia. Nor
in silence.

Naked chrysanthemums from late fall
shiver in cold wind.

Since when do you no longer
relish those brilliant texts, great wisdom
in dictionaries?

More and more your hair looks like dried petals
shivering in cold wind!

(Translated by Fiona Sze-Lorrain)

19 影子

在一座深秋的樹林裏
我和一棵紫楝樹向前奔走
和整座樹林　低矮的灌木叢
一條從容彎曲的水溝
我和厚厚的樹葉迅速移動
拖著長長的影子——

不能想像沒有陰影的事物
一座房屋有它背陰處灰色的
面孔。一張紙有薄而光滑的
脊骨。字，它的影子
　　——相反的詞。
在令人放心的陰影處

有存在　那最安全的保證
是肉眼可見的世界的完整
　　——既不在全然的黑暗
也不在全然的可怖的光中——

Shadow

In late autumn woods
I race alongside a chinaberry tree
and the whole woods   short shrubs
a calm meandering gully
I move swiftly with thick leaves
dragging long shadows—

What is matter without shadow
Every house has its shady gray
face. A piece of paper, its thin glossy
spine. Word, its shadow
      —the antonym.
In the reassuring shade

exists   the surest guarantee
a world's integrity seen by the naked eye
      —neither in sheer dark
nor in sheer ghastly light—

(Translated by Fiona Sze-Lorrain)

20 詩人的工作

一整夜，鐵匠鋪裏的火
呼呼燃燒著。

影子掄圓胳膊，把那人
一寸一寸砸進
鐵砧的沉默。

A Poet's Work

All night long, a fire in the forge
burns and howls.

A shadow frees its arms, pounding the man
inch by inch
into the silence of the anvil.

(Translated by Fiona Sze-Lorrain)

藍藍，1967年出生於山東煙台，中國有影響力的抒情詩人之一。出版有詩歌多部，其中包括《含笑終生》(1990)、《內心生活》(1997)、《睡夢 睡夢》(2003)、《從這裏，到這裏》(2010)；並出版了散文和兒童文學多部。她的作品被翻譯成十種語言。獲得1996年度劉麗安詩歌獎，被選為中國「女詩人十佳」。2009年獲得四項中國詩歌獎：「詩歌與人」詩人獎、「中國十佳詩人獎」、「宇龍詩歌獎」和「冰心兒童文學新作獎」。她多次參加國際詩歌節，現居北京。

Born in 1967 in Yantai, Shandong province, **Lan Lan** is considered one of today's most influential Chinese lyrical poets. She is the bestselling author of several poetry titles including *Life with a Smile* (1990), *Inner Life* (1997), *Dream, Dream* (2003), and *From Here, to Here* (2010). Also a prolific prose and children's fiction writer, her work has been translated into ten languages. Awarded the Liu Li'an Poetry Prize in 1996, she was voted the top writer of the "Best Ten Women Poets" in China. In 2009, she received four of China's highest literary honors: the "Poetry & People" Award, the Yulong Poetry Prize, the "Best Ten Poets in China" Award, and the Bing Xin Children's Literature New Work Award. A regular guest at international poetry festivals, she lives in Beijing.

出版 Publisher
香港中文大學出版社 The Chinese University Press

封面影像 Cover Image
北島 Bei Dao

出版日期 Date of Publication
二零一三年十一月 November 2013

國際書號 ISBN
978-962-996-627-0

香港國際詩歌之夜 2013 International Poetry Nights in Hong Kong 2013
主辦單位 Organizers
香港中文大學文學院 Faculty of Arts, The Chinese University of Hong Kong
香港浸會大學文學院 Faculty of Arts, Hong Kong Baptist University
香港科技大學人文社會科學學院 School of Humanities and Social Science, The Hong Kong University of Science and Technology

合作夥伴 In Partnership With
英國文化協會 British Council

協辦單位 Co-organizers
時刻文化 Moment Communications
香港中文大學出版社 The Chinese University Press

贊助 Sponsors
香港兆基創意書院 HKICC Lee Shau Kee School of Creativity
中國會 The China Club
周凱旋基金會 Chau Hoi Shuen Foundation

Printed in Hong Kong